THE MAKING OF THE MODERN WORLD

1945 TO THE PRESENT

Migration and Refugees

BOOKS IN THE SERIES

Culture and Customs in a Connected World

Education, Poverty, and Inequality

Food, Population, and the Environment

Governance and the Quest for Security

Health and Medicine

Migration and Refugees

Science and Technology

Trade, Economic Life, and Globalization

Women, Minorities, and Changing Social Structures

THE MAKING OF THE MODERN WORLD

1945 TO THE PRESENT

Migration and Refugees

John Perritano

SERIES ADVISOR
Ruud van Dijk

Mason Crest

Mason Crest
450 Parkway Drive, Suite D
Broomall, PA 19008
www.masoncrest.com

© 2017 by Mason Crest, an imprint of National Highlights, Inc. All rights reserved. No part of this publication may be reproduced or transmitted in any form or by any means, electronic or mechanical, including photocopying, recording, taping, or any information storage and retrieval system, without permission from the publisher.

Produced and developed by MTM Publishing.
www.mtmpublishing.com

President and Project Coordinator: Valerie Tomaselli
Designer: Sherry Williams, Oxygen Design Group
Copyeditor: Lee Motteler, GeoMap Corp.
Editorial Coordinator: Andrea St. Aubin
Proofreader: Peter Jaskowiak

ISBN: 978-1-4222-3640-6
Series ISBN: 978-1-4222-3634-5
Ebook ISBN: 978-1-4222-8284-7

Library of Congress Cataloging-in-Publication Data
On file

Printed and bound in the United States of America.

First printing
9 8 7 6 5 4 3 2 1

QR CODES AND LINKS TO THIRD PARTY CONTENT
You may gain access to certain third party content ("Third Party Sites") by scanning and using the QR Codes that appear in this publication (the "QR Codes"). We do not operate or control in any respect any information, products or services on such Third Party Sites linked to by us via the QR Codes included in this publication, and we assume no responsibility for any materials you may access using the QR Codes. Your use of the QR Codes may be subject to terms, limitations, or restrictions set forth in the applicable terms of use or otherwise established by the owners of the Third Party Sites. Our linking to such Third Party Sites via the QR Codes does not imply an endorsement or sponsorship of such Third Party Sites, or the information, products or services offered on or through the Third Party Sites, nor does it imply an endorsement or sponsorship of this publication by the owners of such Third Party Sites.

Contents

Series Introduction 6
CHAPTER 1: The Present Replays the Past 9
CHAPTER 2: World War II and Its Aftermath 17
CHAPTER 3: The Pull of Economic Recovery. 25
CHAPTER 4: The Cold War, Refugees, and Dissidents 33
CHAPTER 5: Natural Disasters, the Environment, and Human Distress 41
CHAPTER 6: The Current Scene. 49
Timeline 56
Further Research. 59
Index. 60
Photo Credits 63
About the Author and Advisor 64

KEY ICONS TO LOOK FOR:

Words to understand: These words with their easy-to-understand definitions will increase the reader's understanding of the text while building vocabulary skills.

Sidebars: This boxed material within the main text allows readers to build knowledge, gain insights, explore possibilities, and broaden their perspectives by weaving together additional information to provide realistic and holistic perspectives.

Educational Videos: Readers can view videos by scanning our QR codes, providing them with additional educational content to supplement the text. Examples include news coverage, moments in history, speeches, iconic sports moments and much more!

Text-dependent questions: These questions send the reader back to the text for more careful attention to the evidence presented there.

Research projects: Readers are pointed toward areas of further inquiry connected to each chapter. Suggestions are provided for projects that encourage deeper research and analysis.

Series Introduction

In 1945, at the end of World War II, the world had to start afresh in many ways. The war had affected the entire world, destroying cities, sometimes entire regions, and killing millions. At the end of the war, millions more were displaced or on the move, while hunger, disease, and poverty threatened survivors everywhere the war had been fought.

Politically, the old, European-dominated order had been discredited. Western European democracies had failed to stop Hitler, and in Asia they had been powerless against imperial Japan. The autocratic, militaristic Axis powers had been defeated. But their victory was achieved primarily through the efforts of the Soviet Union—a communist dictatorship—and the United States, which was the only democracy powerful enough to aid Great Britain and the other Allied powers in defeating the Axis onslaught. With the European colonial powers weakened, the populations of their respective empires now demanded their independence.

The war had truly been a global catastrophe. It underlined the extent to which peoples and countries around the world were interconnected and interdependent. However, the search for shared approaches to major, global challenges in the postwar world—symbolized by the founding of the United Nations—was soon overshadowed by the Cold War. The leading powers in this contest, the United States and the Soviet Union, represented mutually exclusive visions for the postwar world. The Soviet Union advocated collectivism, centrally planned economies, and a leading role for the Communist Party. The United States sought to promote liberal democracy, symbolized by free markets and open political systems. Each believed fervently in the promise and justice of its vision for the future. And neither thought it could compromise on what it considered vital interests. Both were concerned about whose influence would dominate Europe, for example, and to whom newly independent nations in the non-Western world would pledge their allegiance. As a result, the postwar world would be far from peaceful.

As the Cold War proceeded, peoples living beyond the Western world and outside the control of the Soviet Union began to find their voices. Driven by decolonization, the developing world, or so-called Third World, took on a new importance. In particular, countries in these areas were potential allies on both sides of the Cold War. As the newly independent peoples established their own identities and built viable states, they resisted the sometimes coercive pull of the Cold War superpowers, while also trying to use them for their own ends. In addition, a new Communist China, established in 1949 and the largest country in the developing world, was deeply entangled within the Cold War contest between communist and capitalist camps. Over the coming decades, however, it would come to act ever more independently from either the United States or the Soviet Union.

During the war, governments had made significant strides in developing new technologies in areas such as aviation, radar, missile technology, and, most ominous, nuclear energy. Scientific and technological breakthroughs achieved in a military context held promise for civilian applications, and thus were poised to contribute to recovery and, ultimately, prosperity. In other fields, it also seemed time for a fresh start. For example, education could be used to "re-educate" members of aggressor nations and further Cold War agendas, but education could also help more people take advantage of, and contribute to, the possibilities of the new age of science and technology.

For several decades after 1945, the Cold War competition seemed to dominate, and indeed define, the postwar world. Driven by ideology, the conflict extended into politics, economics, science and technology, and culture. Geographically, it came to affect virtually the entire world. From our twenty-first-century vantage point, however, it is clear that well before the Cold War's end in the late 1980s, the world had been moving on from the East-West conflict.

Looking back, it appears that, despite divisions—between communist and capitalist camps, or between developed and developing countries—the world after 1945 was growing more and more interconnected. After the Cold War, this increasingly came to be called "globalization." People in many different places faced shared challenges. And as time went on, an awareness of this interconnectedness grew. One response by people in and outside of governments was to seek common approaches, to think and act globally. Another was to protect national, local, or private autonomy, to keep the outside world at bay. Neither usually existed by itself; reality was generally some combination of the two.

Thematically organized, the nine volumes in this series explore how the post–World War II world gradually evolved from the fractured ruins of 1945, through the various crises of the Cold War and the decolonization process, to a world characterized by interconnectedness and interdependence. The accounts in these volumes reinforce each other, and are best studied together. Taking them as a whole will build a broad understanding of the ways in which "globalization" has become the defining feature of the world in the early twenty-first century.

However, the volumes are designed to stand on their own. Tracing the evolution of trade and the global economy, for example, the reader will learn enough about the political context to get a broader understanding of the times. Of course, studying economic developments will likely lead to curiosity about scientific and technological progress, social and cultural change, poverty and education, and more. In other words, studying one volume should lead to interest in the others. In the end, no element of our globalizing world can be fully understood in isolation.

The volumes do not have to be read in a specific order. It is best to be led by one's own interests in deciding where to start. What we recommend is a curious, critical stance throughout the study of the world's history since World War II: to keep asking questions about the causes of events, to keep looking for connections to deepen your understanding of how we have gotten to where we are today. If students achieve this goal with the help of our volumes, we—and they—will have succeeded.

—Ruud van Dijk

WORDS TO UNDERSTAND

assimilation: process of becoming part of something.

asylum: governmental protection given to a person who has fled another country.

discriminated: treated unequally based on race, ethnicity, gender, or other perceived difference.

genocide: deliberate and systematic extermination of a racial, political, religious, or cultural group.

refugees: people who seek refuge in another country to avoid war, famine, or persecution.

ABOVE: A makeshift refugee camp for Syrians arriving on the Greek island of Kos in September 2015.

CHAPTER

1

The Present Replays the Past

The first photo is beyond disturbing: a small boy, lifeless and face down on a beach in Turkey, his red T-shirt pulled up to the middle of his stomach. His hair looks as if it has just been neatly cut. Over the child's body stands a Turkish police officer, his back to the camera. A second photo shows the same officer holding the dead child and carrying him away.

By day's end, the photos have made their way around the world. People soon learn the boy with the neatly cropped hair is three-year-old Aylan Kurdi, a passenger on one of two overcrowded boats that sailed from Turkey to the Greek island of Kos. Twenty-three people were aboard the boats, including Aylan's older brother, father, and mother. All were **refugees** from Syria trying to reach Europe. Aylan and his family had plans to travel to Canada, where an aunt was waiting.

It was not to be. A wave struck the boat and the family fell overboard into the rough waters of the Aegean Sea. Aylan's father survived, only to learn the rest of his family had perished. They were among the hundreds of thousands of refugees fleeing war-torn Syria during the summer of 2015.

The publication of the haunting photos jolted several countries into action. Within days, the governments of the United States, Germany, Great Britain, and France offered to take in thousands of Syrian refugees, all of whom were trying to escape a bloody civil war. Members of the European Union quickly met to discuss a unified **asylum** policy for the entire continent. "You see a dead child and can't help but be catapulted into action," Caryl M. Stern, president and chief executive of the United States Fund for UNICEF, told the *New York Times*.

By the summer of 2015, six hundred refugees were arriving each night on the tiny island of Kos, making the 2.5-mile (4.1-km) passage across the Aegean Sea. Most came on small boats or rubber rafts owned by smugglers who charged $800 a person for the trip. Other Greek islands, such as Lesbos, were also in the path of this influx.

IN THEIR OWN WORDS

Israeli Politician Isaac Herzog

It is incumbent on Israel to take in refugees from the war and push for the establishment of an urgent international conference on the issue. Jews cannot be apathetic when hundreds of thousands of refugees are searching for safe haven.

– Quoted in the Times of Israel online criticizing the Israeli government's decision to refuse entry to Syrian refugees, September 6, 2015.

In 2014, the Office of the United Nations High Commissioner for Refugees (UNHCR) announced in its Global Trends Report that the number of refugees, asylum-seekers, and those forcibly displaced from their homes had exceeded 50 million for the first time since World War II. The massive spike was driven mainly by the Syrian civil war, which began in 2011. By the summer of 2015, the war had forced more than 4.1 million people to seek safety in other countries, while 7.6 million more were displaced within Syria.

Reminders of the Holocaust

While some governments encouraged the struggling refugees to move to their nations, others, including Hungary, responded by sealing their borders, detaining thousands in makeshift camps, and fighting those that had already arrived with water cannons, dogs, and tear gas.

Collete Avial watched in horror as these and other images played out on television. She couldn't help reliving her nightmare childhood during World War II. As Jews, Avial and her family were forced from their home in Romania by the Nazis. She spent the war years constantly moving and hiding, ultimately surviving the Holocaust that claimed the lives of six million. "I remember running from one place to the other and basically being a refugee," she told CNN. "My sympathy really goes with the refugees, and I do not wish to confine that sympathy to my people alone."

Avial wasn't the only person equating the Syrian refugee crisis with the mass migration of Jews during and after World War II. Many in Israel, a nation founded by Jewish refugees, wanted their government to open its borders to the displaced Syrians. Instead, the government built fences to prevent refugees from crossing into Israel from Jordan, a neighboring country that had taken in close to 750,000 Syrian refugees by the beginning of 2015.

War and Politics

For centuries, people have migrated from one place to another. The reasons for these movements are varied. Some leave voluntarily, searching for a better life. Others move simply to survive. War has been a leading factor, especially in the post–World War II world.

A man outside the remains of his home in Sarajevo after his neighborhood was destroyed in March of 1996; Sarajevo was still the site of violence and looting three months after the official end of the Bosnian civil war in December 1995.

Political and ethnic tensions, especially in Africa, the Middle East, and southeastern Europe, have fueled many mass migrations. In extreme cases, refugees have tried to escape **genocide** and ethnic cleansing, an attempt by one group to create a racially and ethnically pure area through forced migration and mass murder. For instance, at the end of the Bosnian civil war in 1995, which was part of the larger ethnic conflict in the former Yugoslavia (1991–2000) in southeastern Europe, the number of refugees, including those displaced within the country, numbered 2 million.

Others migrate to escape natural disasters, including volcanic eruptions, earthquakes, floods, and tsunamis. In 2014, 19.3 million people were forced to flee their homes because of climate- and weather-related tragedies and geophysical hazards, according to the Norwegian Refugee Council. And in 2015, severe weather alone affected millions. For example, in June 2015 in the South Asian country of Bangladesh, more than 200,000 people were temporarily displaced by floods and landslides during the region's rainy season.

CHAPTER 1   11

Computer climate models have predicted the gradual increase of Earth's surface temperature, and the projected "global warming" is often blamed on human activities such as the burning of fossil fuels. It has been associated with rising temperatures, flooding, droughts, and the rise of sea levels. These disasters have ravaged entire nations. A reporter for the Environmental Justice Foundation claims that the number of so-called environmental refugees will rise to 150 million by 2050, although some say it could top 200 million.

Economic Reasons

People also flee for economic reasons. When people feel that they cannot better themselves economically in their homeland, they often travel to other nations in search of a better life. They are called migrants or immigrants, as opposed to refugees who must leave to avoid immediate danger to themselves or their families.

Migrant farm workers picking strawberries in central California's Salinas Valley in 2015.

That situation is played out every day in Europe and North America, where rich countries, such as Germany and the United States, are situated next door to poorer nations. People from Mexico and other Latin American nations, for example, often migrate north to the United States seeking jobs and better living conditions. People from Eastern Europe and Asia often move to Germany seeking a paycheck and a new home.

Negative and Positive Impacts

The impact of migration can be huge, not only for migrants and refugees, but for the nations taking them in. In most cases, due to the nature of emerging dangers, many refugees move in large numbers to countries that cannot sustain the additional population. Their presence increases economic, environmental, social, and political tensions.

Unless receiving countries can plan for the influx, refugees compete with local citizens for food, housing, water, land, health care, education, and other social services. The influx of new residents also strains the environment, as the demand for natural resources, including water, fuel, food, and building materials, grows.

Syrian refugee children in a makeshift refugee camp in the Bekaa Valley in Lebanon, May 2013.

CHAPTER 1   **13**

IN THEIR OWN WORDS

Antonio Guterres, United Nations High Commissioner for Refugees

While every refugee's story is different and their anguish personal, they all share a common thread of uncommon courage– the courage not only to survive, but to persevere and rebuild their shattered lives.

– Speaking to the UNHCR staff in 2005 as he officially assumed his duties.

The civil war in Syria is a case in point. The tiny neighboring country of Lebanon has struggled to keep up with refugees from the conflict. As of the end of 2015, there were close to 1.1 million UN-registered refugees from the Syrian civil war in Lebanon, according to the United Nations High Commissioner for Refugees (UNHCR); Lebanon's own population was only 4.4 million in 2011, when the Syrian conflict began. Among other pressures, including infrastructure and sanitation issues, Lebanese efforts to educate school-age refugees have hit obstacles. Despite limitations to its educational system, in September 2015, Lebanon put forth a program to enroll 100,000 children in school. An equal number, however, will not be enrolled, according the country's education minister Elias Bou Saab, who announced the plan. The number of Syrians in public school may soon be greater than that of Lebanese children.

The migrants and refugees themselves often face a backlash from the local population. The newcomers look different, and speak and act differently, from everyone else. These and other reasons conspire to fuel hatred among many natives, making immigrant **assimilation** difficult. Consequently, immigrants are **discriminated** against and often are victims of bias-related crime.

At the same time, refugees and migrants can sometimes have positive effects on the receiving countries. In Europe, for example, the population of many countries is aging and shrinking. Overall, this impacts the number of people entering the workforce. Economists say refugees increase a country's labor force, which can jumpstart a flagging economy. Refugees also bring new skills to a community, such as new farming techniques and technical training lacking in many native populations. Refugees also invigorate a community's culture with new ways of life.

Text-Dependent Questions

1. How many Syrians have left their country to seek safety in other countries?
2. Name the main reasons why people are forced from their homes.
3. Why are refugees an important part of the economies of many nations?

Research Projects

1. Go to the website of the Office of the United Nations High Commissioner for Refugees

   (http://www.unhcr.org/cgibin/texis/vtxpage?page=49e486a76&submit=GO)

   and study the "Statistical Snapshot" for Syria. Create a bar chart using those statistics.

2. Write a report describing how the nations of the world responded to Jewish migration from Europe during and after World War II. Compare and contrast what they did.

Educational Video

World in Focus: South Asia's Floods
Page 11
News report about the 2015 flooding in India, Pakistan, Vietnam, and other countries in the southern part of Asia. Published on YouTube by TRT World.
https://youtu.be/WMsQbjkCr8k.

CHAPTER 1   **15**

WORDS TO UNDERSTAND

collaborators: people who work for an enemy occupying a country.

emigrants: people who move from their native land to live elsewhere.

nationalist: advocating national independence or strong national identity.

quotas: in relation to immigration, the upper limits on the number of immigrants allowed to migrate from a specific country.

repatriated: sent back to one's original country.

ABOVE: The scene in July 1945, when children who had survived the Holocaust arrived by train in a refugee camp in Atlit, Palestine.

CHAPTER 2

World War II and Its Aftermath

The armies of liberation came across the camps one by one: Auschwitz, Dachau, Bergin-Belsen. The stench of the Holocaust, the mass murder of over 6 million Jews and others, was everywhere. The Allied soldiers who had beaten back Adolf Hitler's armies tossed the doors to his concentration camps wide open, but the survivors of the Holocaust had no place to go. In 1933, when Hitler came to power, there were 9.5 million Jews in Europe, according to the U.S. Holocaust Memorial Museum's online encyclopedia; in 1950 there were 3.5 million.

The war also created other refugees. The devastation wrought by the war internally displaced some 60 million in Europe alone as homes and land were destroyed. In Asia, tens of millions of people were forced from their homes, including 100 million Chinese. Even healthy soldiers, returning to their homes, were on the move.

Help for Jewish Refugees

The victorious nations—the United States, France, and Great Britain—worked to resettle the Holocaust survivors left homeless after the war, and the United Nations Relief and Rehabilitation Administration (UNRRA) housed them in hundreds of refugee centers and camps across Europe. Some of these centers were located on the sites of former Nazi death camps, including Bergen-Belsen.

At first, conditions in the camps were crowded. Jews were housed alongside German prisoners and Nazi **collaborators**. Slowly, however, conditions improved, and the Allies moved the Jews into separate camps where they were able to make decisions for themselves.

But the influx of displaced Jews continued through 1946 and 1947, when the International Refugee Organization replaced the UNRRA, as thousands streamed westward from Eastern Europe. Various Jewish agencies, including the American Joint Distribution Committee, tried to help the survivors as best they could. They gave them water, food, and clothing. Others groups provided vocational training.

Many survivors of the Holocaust wanted to leave Europe for good and emigrate to the United States and Great Britain. But in the immediate aftermath of the war, each country enforced strict immigration **quotas**. Many Jewish organizations opted secretly to shuttle thousands of Jews to Palestine, which had been operating as a British "mandate," an oversight arrangement authorized by the League of Nations since 1923. One, the Jewish Brigade Group, which fought with the British during the war, sent ship after ship packed with refugees. In most cases, the British denied the **emigrants** entrance, and many were sent to camps on the island of Cyprus in the Mediterranean Sea.

More needed to be done, and by the end of 1945, U.S. president Harry Truman had seen the human and economic toll the refugee crisis was having on a war-shattered Europe. He ordered the U.S. government to loosen its quota restrictions to anyone who had been uprooted by the Nazis.

More than 40,000 displaced persons, including 28,000 Jews, eventually made their way to the United States at that time. Three years later, Congress passed the Displaced Persons Act, providing 400,000 visas for Europeans displaced by the war. Between 1949 and 1952, an estimated 68,000 more Jews came to the United States.

In May 1948, the Jewish state of Israel was founded in Palestine, in the land bordering the eastern Mediterranean, and thousands of Holocaust survivors made their way to the new nation. By 1953, as many as 170,000 Jewish refugees emigrated to Israel, while others moved to Australia, New Zealand, South America, South Africa, and Mexico. The creation of Israel, however, resulted in its own refugee crisis. When the state was declared, fighting broke out between the new Jewish settlers and the Palestinian population living on the land. By early 1949, some 700,000 Palestinians

Scene at the Bergen-Belsen Concentration Camp after it was liberated in 1945 by Allied forces.

MIGRATION AND REFUGEES

Palestinian refugees fleeing oncoming Israeli troops in Galilee following the establishment of Israel in 1948.

had left their towns and villages, now occupied by Israel, for the neighboring countries of Jordan, Lebanon, and Syria.

Others on the Move

The Jews were part of the 60 million Europeans displaced by World War II as fighting raged from one end of the continent to the other. After Germany's defeat, many nations sought retribution. In Czechoslovakia, for example, more than 2.2 million Germans were forced to leave the country after the government confiscated their property. Some 60,000 Germans had fled from Hungary before the war's end. When combat was over, the country expelled the remaining German population. In Romania, only half of the prewar German population of 780,000 remained in the country. And the loss of territory by Germany in Silesia, part of today's Poland, resulted in massive migration of Germans as well.

While these movements of people were happening, ideological shifts were also taking shape. A rift among former Allies—the United States and Britain on one side and the Soviet Union on the other—led to the Cold War, carving up Europe into spheres of influence. Western Europe was dominated by the United States and the

IN THEIR OWN WORDS

President Harry S. Truman

One of the gravest problems arising from the present world crisis is created by the overpopulation in parts of Western Europe, aggravated by the flight and expulsion of people from the oppressed countries of Eastern Europe. This problem is of great practical importance to us because it affects the peace and security of the free world.

– From his Special Message to the Congress on Aid for Refugees and Displaced Persons, March 24, 1952.

Western democracies, while the Soviets formed a bloc of communist nations in Eastern Europe.

Many of the displaced did not want to live under communist rule. The West took in those that fled the communists. Australia, for instance, was in the throes of a labor shortage and needed new workers. From 1945 to 1975, the Australians welcomed 3 million people, including many from Eastern Europe. Still, by 1951, six years after the end of World War II, 1 million European refugees had yet to find a place to settle.

Flux in India

The war also brought great changes to Asia. Part of the British Empire during the war, India was at a crossroads of migration. It sent some 2.5 million soldiers to the war effort—most leaving for fronts in Europe and North Africa. Soldiers were not the only part of Indian society to contribute: many left their rural lives for urban work in the industrial expansion required for military purposes. India also received migrants from Burma, which fell to the Japanese during the war.

This flux continued after the war, when India won its independence from Britain in 1947, after thirty years of struggle. Unfortunately, as independence neared, religious and ethnic tensions flared between Muslims and Hindus. Muslims living in India feared the Hindu majority would discriminate against them. Therefore, the Muslims—under Muhammad Ali Jinnah, who studied law in London—called for the creation of a second separate nation where Muslims would dominate: Pakistan, originally divided into East and West.

The British agreed, and the "Partition" between India and Pakistan was set in motion. As soon as the borders of the new nations were drawn, millions of Hindus in the newly created country fled to India, while millions of Muslims moved from India to East and West Pakistan. It was one of the largest mass migrations in human history, totaling nearly 12 million people.

Most traveled on foot, but many crowded into railway cars and buses. As Muslims fled along crowded roads toward Pakistan, they were slaughtered by Hindus and Sikhs, members of an Indian religious minority. For their part, Muslims killed both Hindus and Sikhs. About 1 million people from all religions were murdered during the migration. Many others died of disease and malnutrition. The migration divided thousands of families. Homes were destroyed and crops were left to wither and rot.

Refugees and the UN

The newly formed United Nations was forced to confront the issue as the movement of refugees and migrants continued unabated around the world. In response, it created the Office of the United Nations High Commissioner for Refugees on December 14, 1950. The agency's main goal was to coordinate international action to protect the migrants and solve the refugee problem.

A massive gathering of Hindu refugees streaming toward India, in September 1947.

Within six years, the UNHCR was facing its first major crisis after World War II, when the Soviet Union crushed a revolution in Hungary. For weeks, word had spread through Hungary about unrest in several Soviet satellite states, including East Germany and Poland. On October 23, 1956, students and workers in Budapest, the capital of Hungary, held a demonstration in support of the Polish protest movement.

Word filtered outward across the city, turning the small protest into a spontaneous national uprising. Tens of thousands poured into the streets. What started as a small demonstration turned into a full-scale revolt against the Soviet Union. On November 4, Soviet tanks and troops poured into the country, crushing the rebellion. Thousands were killed, and 250,000 Hungarians fled the country. Nearly 180,000 poured into nearby Austria and 20,000 more flooded into Yugoslavia.

The UN's response helped shape the way it would respond to future refugee situations. Within days after the Soviet crackdown, the Austrians, the UN, and other resettlement agencies found ways to care for the refugees and quickly resettle them in other countries. It was chaotic at first, but the escaping Hungarians were able to move by boat, train, and plane to thirty-seven different nations, including the United States, which took in nearly 40,000 refugees. Refugees also settled in Canada, Great Britain, West Germany, and Australia.

Africa's Refugee Crisis

After World War II, the colonial powers of Europe were in a state of decline. The British lost India, while some, such as France and Belgium, found it especially difficult to maintain their colonies in Africa. **Nationalist** movements led to independence

UNHCR MANDATE

When the UNHCR was established, the UN General Assembly gave the agency a three-year mandate to help resettle Europe's refugees left homeless by World War II. As the crisis in Europe lessened, other parts of the world were severely affected by their own refugee problems. Consequently, the General Assembly had to keep extending the UNHCR's mandate every five years. Today, the UNHCR has no time constraints.

for many African nations. As a result, ethnic and religious groups that had nothing in common and often mistrusted one another were given the task of nation-building. These differences often led to political instability and war.

In the post–World War II era, tens of thousands of African refugees left their homes to flee ethnic, economic, and religious strife. Many of these mass migrations occurred in Rwanda, Burundi, and other countries in the Great Lakes region of central Africa.

Dealing with the African refugee crises was more problematic than dealing with Europe's refugees. For one thing, the refugees in Africa were moving to nearby countries that were politically unstable. Also, the neighboring countries were not economically prepared. By the end of the 1960s, the United Nations provided most of the help in dealing with the African refugee crisis. In fact, most of the money in the UNHCR's global budget at that time was spent on the continent.

Even more politically stable countries, such as Tunisia and Morocco, felt the pressure. In 1962, Algeria secured its independence from France after a lengthy war. Thousands of refugees swarmed into Tunisia and Morocco, living in tent cities in the desert. The UNHCR, along with the Red Cross, the United States, and others, provided food, clothing, and medicine to the refugees. When the war finally ended and Algeria gained its independence, tens of thousands were **repatriated** from Morocco and Tunisia.

Street scene, with destroyed Soviet tanks, in Budapest during the Hungarian Uprising of 1956.

Text-Dependent Questions

1. How many people were displaced by World War II?
2. Explain how Pakistan was created.
3. When was the UNHCR established?

Research Projects

1. Create a computer slide show that describes the liberation of the Nazi concentration camps at the end of World War II and the resettlement of some of the Holocaust survivors in Israel. Make sure you use photos, maps, and primary source material to tell the story.
2. Use the Internet and the library to create a visual timeline of the various mass migrations that have taken place since the end of World War II.

Educational Video

UNRRA Delivery in 1945
Page 17
Archival footage of Canadian trucks being transported across Europe for the use of the United Nation's Relief and Rehabilitation Administration (UNRRA) in delivering food to war refugees.
Published on YouTube by HuntleyFilmArchives.
https://youtu.be/Y4JDvvPVJeQ.

New equipment for the auto industry in Italy was part of the Marshall Plan, which helped to stimulate employment in Western Europe.

WORDS TO UNDERSTAND

agrarian: relating to the land and farming.

bulwark: something that protects or supports.

capitalism: economic system based on the private ownership of the production and distribution of goods.

existential: relating to the existence and survival of a person or entity.

insurgents: rebels fighting against a political leader or government.

nationalized: take over by the state.

CHAPTER 3

The Pull of Economic Recovery

War had shattered Europe, but the western part of the continent under the influence of the United States, Great Britain, and France was quickly rebuilding its economy. Part of the reason for this resurgence was Europe's location as the epicenter of the Cold War. The Western allies feared that if the United States did not take a more active role in rebuilding the region, the Soviets would ultimately control all of Europe.

Perhaps no one understood this better than Secretary of State George C. Marshall. As the Soviets slowly consolidated power in Poland, the Balkans, East Germany, and all across Eastern Europe, Marshall unveiled what he hoped would be a **bulwark** against communist expansion: an economic plan to rebuild Western Europe.

West Germany benefited most. Between 1950 and 1959, Germany's gross domestic product—the value of all goods and services produced in the country—rose 8 percent each year, faster than anywhere else in Europe. The reasons West Germany's economy grew rapidly were varied. In addition to aid from the West, Germany's economic success could also be traced to its social market economy, a form of **capitalism** in which the government protects the competitive environment from monopolies, while also protecting consumers, workers, and others. Its expansive transportation system, including its highways, canals, and railroads, also fostered economic success. These systems linked every part of the country, allowing companies to move goods around the world.

An Attractive Place

Germany's emergence as an economic power made it a beacon for those looking to better their economic lives. For the first five years after the war, nearly 12 million refugees flocked to West Germany. Many were ethnic Germans who had lived before the war in Poland, Czechoslovakia, Hungary, and Yugoslavia. Between 1945 and 1961, the year the Berlin Wall was constructed, some 3.8 million East Germans moved to West Germany. Many of these migrants were well educated, and this loss of knowledge and skills would result in an **existential** crisis for East Germany.

Germany's highway system, called the Autobahn, was started before World War II. Though much of it was damaged during the fighting, West Germany started to rebuild it soon after the war. In the 1950s, the system expanded, becoming one of the symbols of the country's postwar revitalization.

All came in search of better economic lives. Workers from Turkey were one group of economic migrants that benefited from Germany's success. In 1961, Germany and Turkey signed a labor recruitment agreement as a way for Germany to increase the number of workers that would help keep its economy booming. The Turks were more than happy to leave the poverty of their homeland. After passing fitness tests and receiving vaccinations, hundreds of thousands of Turks boarded special trains for their trek to Germany. The workers arrived and then fanned out across the country. Most of were between eighteen and forty-five years old.

Between 1955 and 1973, 14 million so-called guest workers came to Germany from Italy, Morocco, and Portugal, although Turkey contributed the majority. Germany depended heavily on these guest workers, but the government never intended the immigrants to stay. It did not provide them with a path to citizenship, leading to mistrust on both sides. In time, the Turks formed the largest ethnic minority in Germany, with nearly 2.7 million people.

Moving across Europe

Germany was not the only European country that opened its doors to economic migrants in the postwar world. Independence struggles in Africa created a flood of migrants into the former colonial powers of France, Great Britain, the Netherlands, and Belgium. Civil servants who had worked for the colonial governments, along with soldiers and European settlers, emigrated from the former colonies to the "motherlands." Others were forced to leave because of civil war, political unrest, and religious and ethnic persecution.

Many of those who traveled to Great Britain came from India and Pakistan, while France saw an influx of Algerians, Tunisians, and Moroccans. France also received migrants from Vietnam as its influence in Indochina waned. The migration was a boon to many European nations, which during the 1950s and 1960s were dealing with a labor shortage. As governments actively recruited migrants from other nations as well, the influx of foreigners continued well into the 1970s.

Eventually, migration among several European countries was made easier by the Schengen Agreement, which affected border control and visa policies across five of the ten members of the European Union, then called the European Economic Community. Signed on June 14, 1985, near the town of Schengen in Luxemburg, the agreement made it easier for migrants to move from one country to another. The agreement, for instance, created a common visa, which made travel much easier. Those borders would truly be opened under the European Union's Maastricht Treaty, signed in 1992.

Mexican Workers in the United States

The United States during the early Cold War years also found itself as a haven for millions of economic migrants, most coming from Latin America. When World War II began, the United States was faced with a severe labor shortage as many American men went to war. Consequently, the government began rethinking its immigration policies. U.S. employers pressured the federal government to approach Mexico in the hopes of securing more workers. The result was the Bracero Program, which brought millions of Mexican guest workers to the United States (*bracer* is a Spanish term that loosely means "one who works with his arms").

Many of those coming to the United States were poor. Each laborer had to sign a contract to work in the country. During the war, an average of 70,000 contract laborers moved north. The program was very successful, and by 1949 the number of braceros had jumped to 113,000. Between 1950 and 1954, more than 200,000 Mexican workers came to the United States on average each year. When the program ended in 1964, 4.6 million braceros had arrived.

The program did have its controversial points. Those Mexicans desperate for work took the most grueling jobs. Mexican farmworkers already living in the United States

Mexican workers recruited by the Farm Security Administration in 1943 to help fill the shortage of agricultural workers resulting from the war.

were worried that the new migrants would compete for jobs and wages. Furthermore, employers often ignored the rules of the program. Companies were supposed to provide workers with adequate wages, clean facilities, free housing, and decent, inexpensive meals, along with free transportation back to Mexico at the end of the contract period. Many employers did not follow these rules, refusing to spend a lot of money on this plentiful pool of cheap labor.

The program also increased unauthorized Mexican migration for braceros who could not secure contracts under the Bracero Program. These workers were drawn to the United States because wages were nearly ten times higher than in Mexico. The number of unauthorized Mexicans coming into the United States increased from 91,000 in 1946 to 500,000 in 1951.

Migration from Cuba and Elsewhere

From the late 1950s through the 1980s, political and economic turmoil in Cuba and other Latin American countries spurred migration to the United States. In 1959, left-wing political **insurgents** led by Fidel Castro and Ernesto Ché Guevara overthrew Cuba's dictatorial government.

The revolution upended the political, social, and economic structures of the island, as Cuba became a Marxist state. Castro **nationalized** key industries, forcing a mass exodus of Cubans. Around 71,000 Cuban refugees left the island for the United States in 1950. Ten years later, the Cuban immigrant population in the United States had increased to 163,000.

Fidel Castro

During the next ten years, several waves of Cuban immigration occurred. By 1970, the Cuban population in the United States had reached 638,000. In the 1980s, another 125,000 Cubans entered the country during the so-called Mariel Boatlift. The boatlift acted as a pressure release for a country with too few jobs and not enough housing. On April 20, 1980, Castro allowed all Cubans wishing to emigrate to the United States to board boats in the port city of Mariel, as long as they had someone to pick them up. Relatives in the United States scurried to hire boats to rescue their relatives. Castro also opened the boatlift to prisoners, many of whom were common criminals, but also included were many who had been jailed for their political beliefs and activities. The exodus ended in October.

Economic and political turmoil elsewhere in Latin America also contributed to an increase in migration. During this period, the average income for Latin American

OPERATION BOOTSTRAP

In 1947, Puerto Rico's government began an industrial program: Operación Manos a la Obra, or Operation Bootstrap. The goal was to transform Puerto Rico, an American territory, from an **agrarian**-based economy to an industrialized society that lifted people out of poverty. The program was a failure. Chronic unemployment hovered between 10.4 and 20 percent from 1949 to 1977. Consequently, Puerto Rican immigration to the United States skyrocketed.

workers was 12 percent lower than the average income for American workers. In addition, economic growth in Latin America was habitually low. The region's growing population strained Latin America's fragile economies even further. Although the United States had its own economic problems during this period, many Latin Americans still believed they could find a better life in the north.

In 1965 Castro allowed Cubans wishing to migrate to the United States to leave from the port of Camarioca. Pictured here are Cubans arriving in Key West, Florida, during that period.

Text-Dependent Questions

1. How many refugees fled to West Germany at the end of World War II, and where did most of them come from?
2. What was the Bracero Program?
3. How many Cubans entered the United States during the Mariel Boatlift?

Research Project

Almost everyone in the United States is an immigrant or is descended from an immigrant. Break off into groups of five or six. Go around the table and have each person describe their family's heritage. Ask questions such as: What country were you born in? Where did your parents come from? Where did your grandparents come from? Where did your great-grandparents come from? How did they get here? Why did they leave their original home? Find out as much detail as possible. Take notes, and then give an oral report to the rest of the class on what you discovered.

WORDS TO UNDERSTAND

armistice: agreement between countries to end a conflict.

demilitarized: officially cleared of soldiers or military personnel of any kind.

dissidents: people who disagree with an established political system.

exodus: massive departure or emigration.

ideology: system of beliefs, values, and ideas that a person can live by and that can form the basis of a society.

ABOVE: A Korean family seeks safety in a refugee camp near Masan, South Korea, in 1950 at the start of the Korean War.

CHAPTER 4

The Cold War, Refugees, and Dissidents

The Cold War would stimulate various waves of migrations during its long history. One of the most prominent examples began in 1950 on the Korean Peninsula—one of the first epicenters of contact between communist and Western capitalist forces in the Cold War. The Korean War began when North Korea, supported by China (which was in turn helped by the Soviet Union), attacked South Korea, supported by the United States and its allies in the United Nations. In 1953, the UN, North Korea, and China signed an **armistice** establishing a 150-mile-long **Demilitarized** Zone (DMZ) that neither side could cross.

Even before the war, North Koreans had been heading south, and the war created even more reason to flee. In all, between 1945 and 1953, some 900,000 North Koreans, roughly 10 percent of the population, left the country. The division separated families and friends, while displacing many people from their homes. The DMZ also created a physical barrier against voluntary repatriation: those who wanted to return to their homes could not cross it.

To complicate matters, 300,000 Chinese, many of whom were soldiers, stayed in North Korea. The Chinese government wanted them back. For their part, North Korea's leaders asked the Chinese to send back some 400,000 ethnic Koreans then living in China. In addition, many North Korean prisoners of war did not return to their homes after the armistice was signed. Instead, they traveled to Chile and Argentina in South America. The entire region was on the move.

Opening the Doors

South Korea at the time had no problem opening its borders to the influx of refugees. By law, North Koreans were entitled to South Korean citizenship and were admitted under a policy that provided the refugees with job training, health-care services, and financial help.

Soldiers manning the observation point in the Demilitarized Zone on the border looking from South Korea to North Korea.

After the war, South Korea, with the help of the United States and to some extent Japan, prospered and modernized. People found jobs building ships, cars, trucks, and televisions. At the same time, North Korea turned inward, isolating itself from the rest of the world, resulting in a life of poverty for most of its citizens. But the government of North Korea refused to allow its citizens to emigrate. Only a handful of North Koreans were able slip into the South. In fact, only about 20,000 people left North Korea in the last twenty years or so. Despite the fact that China often sends escapees back in fear of setting off the collapse of North Korea, many have escaped by going to work in China and then moving on to South Korea.

Dissidents

At the end of World War II, thousands of Soviets left their homeland in search of political, economic, educational, and artistic freedom. Many artists, writers, and scientists emigrated to the United States and the West, and by 1952, the Soviets had become so embarrassed by the mass **exodus** that they established heavy-handed controls over emigration.

Anyone who defected became a "nonperson" in the eyes of the Soviet government. Communist officials refused to allow the defectors to contact their families, and in many cases it was illegal to mention the defector's name. Many that left were **dissidents** that not only disagreed with Soviet society and political **ideology**, but were also willing to speak out against the abuses of the government. One of the most vocal—and internationally well-known—dissidents was Aleksandr Solzhenitsyn, who was exiled under the sentence of treason, following the publication outside of the Soviet Union of *The Gulag Archipelago* in 1974.

Classical dancers and musicians, along with other artists and intellectuals, were drawn by the artistic freedom in the West. Best known perhaps is the Soviet dancer Mikhail Baryshnikov, who many consider one of the greatest male ballet dancers of the twentieth century. He defected in 1974, years after another great Russian dancer, Rudolf Nureyev, had done so while on tour in Paris in 1961. The classical pianist and conductor Vladimir Feltsman applied for an exit visa in 1979 and, in addition to being denied, was banned from performing publicly in the Soviet Union. The government gave in eight years later, and Feltsman was able to leave Russia.

Of course, it worked the other way as well. Western intelligence agents, for instance, spying for Eastern Bloc countries, would often seek asylum in the Eastern Bloc. However, West-to-East defections were much fewer and much less visible.

ISLANDS OF NO RETURN

Soviet gulags were a system of forced-labor camps, in which millions of people suffered and died, although many did not commit any crimes. Most succumbed to hunger and cold. One of the gulag's most famous residents was Aleksandr Solzhenitsyn, a writer, historian, and outspoken critic of the Soviet regime. In his book, *The Gulag Archipelago*, Solzhenitsyn describes—within the context of the four-decade history of the Soviet gulag system—his time in the camps along with that of fellow prisoners.

Refuseniks

The simmering conflict between Israel and the neighboring Arab countries of Egypt, Jordan, and Syria erupted into the Six-Day War in June of 1967. Following the Arab defeat, after which Israel gained territory equal to one-third of its original size, Jews in the Soviet Union began voicing their support for the Jewish state. Soviet leaders tried to quash their opinions, arresting many and sentencing some to long prison terms in the gulags of Siberia.

Crowds celebrate the unification of Berlin on the twenty-fifth anniversary of the fall of the Berlin Wall in 2014.

After the war, many Jews applied for visas to move to Israel. Although a few left, the Soviets refused to allow most Jews to emigrate, resulting in the term "refuseniks." As soon as the Jews requested permission to leave, they were fired from their jobs and lost all means of income in the Soviet state-run economy. By the 1990s, as the Soviet Union became more open, the government allowed many refuseniks to leave.

Fall of the Berlin Wall

The Berlin Wall had divided East and West Germany since 1961. The communists erected it to keep East Germans from escaping to the democratic West. For nearly thirty years, the wall stood as a monument to oppression and a symbol of Cold War tensions.

By the fall of 1989, however, communism began to implode as the liberalizing policies of Soviet premier Mikhail Gorbachev began to be tested by the peoples of Eastern and Central Europe. On November 9, 1989, East Germany announced it would open its border and allow its citizens to travel freely to the West. The next day, thousands of Berliners flocked to the wall and began slowly taking it down. And by 1990, Germany was once again a unified nation.

At first, assimilating was difficult. West Germany absorbed tens of thousands of workers and tried to provide them with jobs. The nation struggled, but things slowly got better. In 2013, officials in Germany declared that the westward migration was over, with only 2,000 people leaving the old East Germany the year before. Between 1990 and 2013, the population of the west had grown by 6.7 percent, while the population of the east had dropped 13.5 percent.

"Boat People"

After Japan was defeated in World War II, the French regained control of their former colony in Vietnam. But Vietnam's communist leader, Ho Chi Minh, began a drive for independence. After the Vietnamese defeated the French in 1954, a peace conference held in Geneva granted independence to Vietnam, Laos, and Cambodia, but Vietnam was divided into two states on the insistence of the United States. The communists ruled the north, while a noncommunist government was elected in the south. Unwilling to accept the national elections agreed upon in 1954, South Vietnamese president Ngo Dinh Diem, supported by the Americans, in 1956 laid the basis for a new war. The United States replaced France, and eventually found itself mired in one of the longest and most unpopular war in its history. In April 1975, after years of anti–Vietnam War protests, the United States ended its involvement in Vietnam, paving the way for the North Vietnamese to take over South Vietnam.

The switch in government and the forcible relocation of tens of thousands of people into "reeducation camps" and "economic zones" created a massive humanitarian crisis. Tens of thousands of refugees scrambled to leave Vietnam, boarding whatever type of boat they could find. They crowded into these makeshift vessels and sailed out into the South China Sea toward an uncertain future. Known collectively as the "boat people," the refugees traveled to Hong Kong, Indonesia, Malaysia, the Philippines, Singapore, and Thailand.

On the water, the refugees had to endure storms, diseases, and pirates. The mass departure went on for months. While many found refuge in camps across the region, they strained the resources of many Southeast Asian countries. As the U.S. Navy's Sixth Fleet plucked many escaping Vietnamese from the sea, President Jimmy Carter asked the United Nations to convene a special meeting to solve the crisis. He sent Vice President Walter Mondale to implore the international community for help.

After that meeting, many more nations opened their borders to the boat people. The United States ended up taking in 1 million, while thousands of other refugees found new lives in Canada, Australia, and the United Kingdom. Vietnam also agreed to limit the number of people leaving the country. While most left between 1975 and 1980, the exodus continued through the early 1990s.

Refugees aboard a Vietnamese fishing boat await rescue by the U.S. navy ship *Blue Ridge* in May of 1984.

Text-Dependent Questions

1. How many North Korean refugees were there between 1945 and 1953?
2. What was a "refusenik?"
3. Where did the "boat people" come from, and why did they leave?

Research Projects

1. Write a short biography of either Aleksandr Solzhenitsyn, Mikhail Gorbachev, or Mikhail Baryshnikov.
2. Break off into groups of three or four and brainstorm ways that recent immigrants or refugees have influenced your community. For example, are there specific neighborhoods where refugees live? Are there cultural centers? What types of foreign restaurants are there? Create a list and present your findings to the class.

Destruction caused by Typhoon Haiyan in Tacloban on the island of Leyte in the Philippines.

WORDS TO UNDERSTAND

disseminate: spread or circulate widely, as with ideas or information.

earmarked: set aside for a specific purpose.

greenhouse gas: any of the atmospheric gases that contribute to the greenhouse effect by absorbing infrared radiation produced by solar warming of Earth's surface.

habitat: natural conditions and environment in which plants and animals live.

limbo: condition or state of uncertainty.

tsunamis: massive sea waves caused by underwater earthquakes or eruptions off the coast of a landmass.

CHAPTER

5

Natural Disasters, the Environment, and Human Distress

On November 7, 2013, Typhoon Haiyan blew across the Philippines, causing widespread devastation. Blowing across the islands with wind gusts that topped 171 miles (275 km) per hour, Haiyan killed more than 6,000 people and left tens of thousands homeless.

According to the United Nations, the storm displaced some 4.4 million people, with nearly 500,000 staying in local evacuation centers. Anacleta, a seventy-seven-year-old widow, was one of them. She was living on the side of the road near the ruins of her house two years after the storm. "My family and I were evacuated to a nearby center," Anacleta remembered. "When I returned, I found my house had almost completely collapsed. I've lived there for twenty-five years."

The number of people forced to become refugees because of natural disasters and other environmental events seems to rise every year. According to the Norwegian Refugee Council (NRC), 26.4 million people have been forced to flee their homes because of natural or environmental disasters since 2008—that's one person every second. In 2014, that number was 19.3 million, a grim statistic some predict will grow to 50 million by 2050, owing to the effects of climate change. Most of the displaced in 2014 came from Asia.

Natural Disasters and Humanitarian Relief

Since the end of World War II, the destruction caused by natural disasters and environmental damage has drawn more and more attention from across the world. Globalization, which has connected peoples from different continents and cultures, has helped to **disseminate** information about hurricanes, earthquakes, **tsunamis**, and cyclones at lightning speed. It has also helped to mobilize responses to them.

ENVIRONMENTAL REFUGEES AND THE UN

In 1985, the United Nations Environment Program defined environmental refugees "as those people who have been forced to leave their traditional **habitat**, temporarily or permanently, because of a marked environmental disruption (natural and/or triggered by people) that jeopardized their existence and/or seriously affected the quality of their life." Some of these environmental disruptions include natural events such as hurricanes. They also include displacement due to dam construction, the logging of rain forests, nuclear disasters, and even biological warfare.

Despite this recognition from the UN, the agreement resulting from climate talks in Paris in December 2015 did not officially include a call for a category of "climate refugees," who would be granted the same rights as other types of refugees. Many critics suggest that the hundreds of thousands of people expected to migrate in the coming decades due to drastic environmental changes will be left in a state of international **limbo**.

One of the most devastating natural disasters since World War II was the Bhola cyclone that hit East Pakistan (now Bangladesh) and the east coast of India in 1970. While the exact death toll is not known, some estimates suggest that as many 500,000 died. Whole villages were wiped out, and the number of displaced and homeless will never be known. A massive humanitarian relief effort, one of the largest to that date, was undertaken. CARE International and the United Nations made large donations. The United States **earmarked** $10 million for food and other essentials, Canada offered $2 million, and Japan provided $1.65 million. Involving many other countries, the efforts were made more complex as a result of the strained relationship between Pakistan and India, as well as between Pakistan and other countries.

Such disasters, and the relief efforts that follow, have sadly become commonplace events, and news about them spreads quickly through online media outlets. In 2004, a massive underwater earthquake, the third largest on record, created a huge tsunami that swept across the Indian Ocean. Affecting fourteen countries, it resulted in 228,000 dead or missing and 1.7 million displaced and homeless. Indonesia was the first in the tsunami's path, and the loss of life there was estimated at more than 160,000. Indonesia, India, and Sri Lanka each had over 500,000 displaced. The response was swift and vast, with countries pledging $14 billion dollars in aid to the damaged areas. The United Nations Environment Program set aside $1 million in emergency funds and established a technical task force to help the governments of the regions respond. This scene has played out again and again in various corners of the world. Haiti was struck by a huge earthquake in 2010, with some 160,000 dead and 250,000 homes destroyed. In 2014, floods in Indonesia displaced some 120,000 people.

Even the United States has suffered serious losses. In 2005, Hurricane Katrina devastated large portions of low-lying New Orleans and other cities along the Gulf of Mexico, with the dead and missing numbering close to 2,000. It displaced more than a million people, but by the end of January 2006 about half of the prestorm population had returned to New Orleans. The city's population, however, was still recovering ten years later.

As such events seem to become more commonplace, and certainly more prominent in the media, the relief efforts and humanitarian response—while often swift and vast—fall terribly short. Many policy makers argue that preparation for inevitable disasters must be the focus of national governments and international agencies, especially as environmental pressures, including dire predictions of climate change, increase.

The Change in Climate

One of the most pressing concerns in recent years is the effect that climate change has on human habitat. The planet is slowly warming, which is causing its climate to change. Scientists estimate that Earth's surface temperature has risen about 0.9 degrees Fahrenheit (0.5 degrees Celsius) since the 1800s. Further, scientific research suggests that since the Industrial Revolution, human activities, which include the burning of fossil fuels such as oil and coal, have contributed to a 20 to 30 percent increase in carbon dioxide, a **greenhouse gas** that traps the sun's energy near the Earth's surface, gradually warming the planet.

The 2004 tsunami in Asia caused massive destruction and homelessness in many countries, including in this area in Aceh, Indonesia.

The Funafuti Atoll, part of the Pacific island nation of Tuvalu threatened by rising sea waters.

Climate change is blamed for longer droughts, massive floods, melting ice caps, and rising sea levels. Many believe the results can already be seen. The tiny Pacific nation of Tuvalu, comprised of low-lying atolls, is losing ground quickly to the rising ocean, a fate facing other small island countries. Many of the island's 11,000 residents have already migrated to other nations, including New Zealand and Australia. Scientists predict that in fifty years the island will be completely underwater.

On the island of Shishmaref, Alaska, the sea ice that once protected the small village from damaging floods and storm-driven waves is melting. The changing climate has forced many of the island's residents to leave for the mainland. Many environmental scientists even predict that parts of New York City and areas on the East Coast will eventually be underwater as sea levels rise, as will parts of the European coastline.

Climate Change in Africa

Perhaps no region has been affected more by the environment than Africa. One of the worst situations occurred in the 1980s in Ethiopia, where a massive drought and famine killed tens of thousands. The government responded by forcibly uprooting people and resettling them in the southern part of the country. By 1986, the military had forced 600,000 people to leave their villages and farms. Human rights organizations said tens of thousands died as a result of the government's actions.

Problems with famine and drought continue to intensify in Africa today. Desertification—the process by which human activities and climate changes turn productive land into desert—has been driving thousands of migrants to Europe. The change in climate has also created political and social instability as basic resources, such as water and food, literally dry up. Thousands have tried to move away from regions of crop failure and severe water shortages caused by a changes in rainfall patterns.

Those who leave undertake a treacherous journey north. An estimated 700 Africans drowned in the Mediterranean Sea in April 2015 as they tried to migrate. The refugees aboard a lopsided fishing boat saw a merchant ship in Libyan waters. As they rushed to one side to hail the ship, the fishing boat turned over, tossing the migrants into the water. At the time of the accident, some 1,500 migrants had already died on route to Europe in 2015. Experts estimate that the situation will only get worse, as up to 250 million Africans will suffer from water and food insecurity in the coming years.

The problems are most acute in countries such as Nigeria, which is losing more than 1,350 square miles of land to desertification each year. Lake Chad, which provides water for 25 million people, is drying up, while rainfall in the region is expected to decrease 10 to 20 percent by 2025.

The migrants who arrive in Europe are straining the continent's resources and patience. In June 2015, France and Italy tightened border security, hoping to reduce the inflow of African refugees. Hundreds of people, including families with young children, had to sleep in cramped railway stations after France denied them admission. In Italy, police and migrants in the town of Ventimiglia, on the Mediterranean coast three miles from France, clashed repeatedly over the summer. Stopped from going any further, many families had to sleep on the rocks along the sea.

Drought in the Horn of Africa, at the continent's eastern edge, has destroyed crops and livestock. Seen here is Aden Jama in Somaliland with one of the few remaining goats in his herd in 2012.

ENVIRONMENTAL STRESS IN SYRIA

African migrants are just part of the total number of those streaming into Europe. Many more—in fact most—are coming from the Middle East, especially Syria. A study published in the Proceedings of the National Academy of Scientists cites the role of climate change in the drying and warming of the region over the past century, which in turn has led to more and more severe droughts. One such drought helped to bring about the Syrian civil war, according to the report. Prior to 2011, the study says, several years of severe drought had led to failed harvests, which in turn fueled popular dissatisfaction with President Bashir Assad's rule in that country.

Pope Francis condemned European countries for "closing the door" on the African refugees. He said, according to a report on Daily Mail.com, "These brothers and sisters of ours are seeking refuge far from their lands, they are seeking a home where they can live without fear."

Bangladesh on the Front Lines

Environmental refugees greatly affect neighboring areas as they migrate. Over the years, thousands of people living in Bangladesh, which in many places is less than 33 feet (10 m) above sea level, have had to flee because of storms, floods, and earthquakes. Many moved inland toward neighboring India. Others were forced into overcrowded slums.

Experts predict that Bangladesh's population is expected to balloon to 250 million people by 2050. The monsoon floodwaters that occur annually can inundate two-thirds of the country, possibly forcing 10 to 30 million people to become refugees. Bangladesh will be made even more vulnerable to severe storms as climate change continues to have its effect.

Text-Dependent Questions

1. How many people have been forced to leave their homes because of natural or environmental disasters?
2. Give three examples of "environmental disruption."
3. What is Bangladesh's population estimated to be in 2050?

Research Projects

1. Research and create a chart showing the top five environmental disasters within the last decade, along with the number of people each disaster displaced.
2. Use the Internet and the library to research how environmental refugees from one country have had an effect on other countries. Summarize your findings in a report.

LEFT: This man fishing in a flooded field in Bangladesh is one example of how people in that country have learned to adapt to frequent flooding. With much of its land barely above sea level, however, the people of Bangladesh may have a hard time adapting as sea levels rise in the future.

Syrian refugees behind a barricade on the border between Slovenia and Croatia in September 2015, as a volunteer with the UNHCR waits to assist them.

WORDS TO UNDERSTAND

animates: gives life or inspiration to.

internally displaced person: person forced to leave their home, but seeks refuge in their own country.

moratorium: agreement to delay or halt a planned activity.

notorious: widely known for shameful behavior.

right-wing: characterized by conservative political conviction or temperament.

xenophobia: intense fear or dislike of foreigners.

CHAPTER 6

The Current Scene

After the Turkish police officer had picked up the body of three-year old Aylan Kurdi and taken it away, the boy's father, Abdullah, spoke from a hospital bed detailing his family's struggle as refugees from the Syrian civil war. Abdullah said he and his family witnessed months of bloodshed and violence between the Islamic State (also known as ISIS or ISIL), the terrorist group fighting for territory in Syria and northern Iraq, and Syrian Kurdish forces near the town of Kobani. Now only Abdullah is alive; the rest of the family, in addition to Aylan, was lost when their boat capsized just after setting out from Turkish shores.

The story of Aylan and his family is just one of many told by refugees. In 2005, according to the United Nations, 37.5 million people were displaced by war. That number skyrocketed to 59.5 million in 2014. To put it in perspective, as of this writing, 1 out of every 122 humans is currently a refugee, an **internally displaced person**, or a person seeking asylum. If all those people could gather and form their own country, it would be the twenty-fourth most populous nation in the world.

Officials attribute most of the increase to the Syrian civil war, where every day, on average, 42,000 people are displaced. The magnitude of the current refugee crisis, however, has been intensified by political unrest, famine, and social discord in countries like Ukraine, Afghanistan, and Somalia.

Migration and Globalization

Since the end of World War II, migration has been one of the features and drivers of a new era of globalization. Globalization increases trade, affects economies, and connects governments and individuals. As cultural connections increase and information is freely exchanged across those borders, people's awareness of other ways of life increases as well. This **animates** the immigrant's dream of improving one's chances for a better life.

The receiving countries benefit greatly from these trends, but there are plusses on both sides. As new immigrants fill jobs that native workers can't or won't take, they infuse their adopted countries with energy and new ideas. Adding diversity to a country's ideological or cultural makeup offers more options for everyone.

Economic life is also enriched. For migrants that are easily employed in their new homes, their economic prospects rise. In the process, migrants send cash payments—called "remittances"—back to their families, bringing much-needed income to their home countries. In 2014, remittances to India totaled $70 billion, to China $64 billion, and to the Philippines $28 billion, according to the World Bank's chief economist, Kaushik Basu, who says that such substantial income can "finance development and infrastructure projects." And while immigrants pay taxes in their adopted homes and save a good portion of their salaries, the host country reaps benefits as well.

Globalization also drives "intellectual migration," as people who cannot find an appropriate job in their own country leave. For example, Filipino nurses in recent years have immigrated to the United States to fill vacancies at U.S. hospitals. In fact, in many American hospitals, Filipino nurses make up the majority of the staff. And if their families stay behind, they benefit from remittances sent home, while the U.S. health-care system benefits as well.

Seen from this angle, increased migration under globalization seems like a win-win situation. However, intellectual migration alone can cause problems. It drains

Remittances, sent by immigrants to their families at home, pump cash into the economies of home countries. In many cases, storefront shops such as this in Hong Kong help to manage cash transfers to family members.

the workforce of poor countries, threatening their development. According to the Organisation for Economic Co-operation and Development, a group of thirty-four countries that promotes world trade, half of all university graduates in the poor nations of sub-Saharan Africa and Central America migrate to countries with greater opportunity, such as the United States and the wealthier nations of Europe. This so-called brain drain has especially negative effects in important sectors such as health care, education, and engineering.

Increased migration also might cause strains on infrastructure and social services, problems particularly acute in smaller, less-wealthy receiving countries, such as Lebanon and Jordan during the Syrian civil war. Limited job markets present other issues—in poorer countries but also in developed economies that are experiencing economic downturns such as the economic crises of 2007–2008. Additionally, some migrants will arrive in their adopted countries without the skills and training needed to fit into a country's job market, even when it's healthy. If educational opportunity is available, this lack of preparation might not create stress for the immigrant and might not be a burden on the new country; if unavailable, problems are likely to arise.

> **SENDING MONEY HOME**
>
> The growth rate of remittances to developing countries from 2014 to 2015, at just under 1 percent, was the lowest rate since the 2007-2008 economic crisis, according to the World Bank. Totaling $440 billion in 2015, remittances will begin to increase more quickly in 2016, when the World Bank estimates they will total $459 billion, and the bank estimates a further increase to $479 billion in 2017.

Fortress Europe?

Many countries in the European Union (EU) are of two minds in dealing with the refugee crisis stemming from the Syrian civil war and larger questions connected to economic migration. In Germany, for instance, the government decided to take in more asylum seekers than any other nation in Europe. Mindful of its people's infamous behavior during World War II, when the Nazis tried to exterminate entire classes of people, Germany has been the most welcoming nation in Europe and was expecting to take in at least 800,000 refugees by the end of 2015.

At the same time, the government faces a potential backlash. For instance, the city of Meissen renovated an apartment building in 2015 to house dozens of refugees from Syria and elsewhere. The building had balconies, modern appliances, and a neighborhood pub nearby. Then it burned, set ablaze by **right-wing** arsonists who didn't want to see the foreigners in their community. The fire occurred days before the refugees were to arrive. Refugee centers across Germany had also been targeted, as well as the refugees themselves. Despite this mounting **xenophobia**, the government insisted its policy was the correct, humanitarian response to the refugee crisis.

A CHALLENGE TO EUROPE

In an ironic twist, the refugee crisis poses a serious threat to the EU and European integration, which is considered to be one of the success stories of the post-1945 era. The EU can't seem to devise—let alone implement—common policies on the refugee problem, an issue that by definition is a shared challenge.

RIGHT: Asylum seekers outside the gates of the Consulate of Sweden in Istanbul, Turkey, in October 2015. Sweden has been one of the most open European countries during the recent refugee crisis.

Other smaller countries have followed suit; Sweden, for instance, has taken the most refugees of any country in Europe as a percentage of its population. And it has argued for more openness from its fellow Europeans. While Germany and Sweden argue in support of settlement programs, other nations, including Hungary and Bulgaria, have built walls to keep out the migrants. Slovakia announced it would accept 200 Syrians, but only if they were Christians. France's attitude lies somewhere in between, but their response might be complicated by the November 2015 attacks by Islamic State terrorists in Paris. The far-right, anti-immigrant National Front called for tightening immigration systems immediately following the attacks. Such concerns are spreading to the United States, particularly after the terrorist attacks in San Bernardino, California, in December 2015, which resulted in fourteen deaths. Many see the American openness to the immigrant dream as being directly opposed to the country's security needs.

Backlash in the USA

Days after Aylan Kurdi's body was found on the shores of Turkey, the United States, under increasing political pressure, agreed to take in 10,000 displaced Syrians. Refugee aid groups called the move a token gesture. And indeed, in the past the United States was viewed as a haven for refugees. That all changed after the terrorist attacks on September 11, 2001. Since then, the number of refugees entering the United States has dropped sharply. In 2014, only 69,987 refugees were admitted into the country, compared with 80,000 in one month alone during the 1980 Mariel Boatlift. The Syrian refugee crisis stoked fears among many that the United States was opening itself up to Islamic terrorists, and the December 2015 terrorist attacks by a couple in San Bernardino, one of whom was a recent immigrant, raised more concerns.

In the United States, almost everyone is an immigrant or descended from one. For much of its history, millions came to America looking for a chance to start a new life. Some came to escape wars, others to seek their fortune, or at the very least to make a decent living. Still others came for the freedom to practice their own religion. America did not disappoint and kept its doors open, although restrictions were placed on various groups over the decades. One of the most **notorious** was Chinese Exclusion Act of 1882 that instituted a ten-year **moratorium** on Chinese immigration, which was renewed and made permanent in the following decades.

During the Cold War years, immigration policy in the United States shifted with each decade. In the 1950s and 1960s, access was denied to immigrants who were politically radical and extended to those that were willing to enmesh themselves in the political, cultural, and economic fabric of the United States. In 1965, the Immigration and Nationality Act abolished previous per-nationality quotas, considered to be an embarrassment during the time of the civil rights movement; instead, it favored those with skills needed to fill gaps in the labor pool and those with existing family connections in the United States. By 1978, Congress had passed amendments to the immigration law, setting a worldwide limit of 290,000 immigrants. By the late 1980s, unauthorized aliens were given the opportunity to gain legal status if they met certain criteria.

A political cartoon criticizing the Chinese Exclusion Act of 1882.

In more recent years, however, the United States has been trying to navigate its way through thorny political debates as the government rethinks its immigration policy. Sometimes the discussions have become racist and xenophobic, as various groups and individuals blame undocumented workers for a variety of ills that they claim are ruining American society and harming its economy. While it's true that the population of unauthorized immigrants ballooned during the 1990s, it peaked at 12.2 million in 2007. Those numbers then dropped sharply between 2007 and 2009 and have continued to decrease, dispelling the notion that the country is being overrun by hordes of foreigners.

Another misconception is that unauthorized immigrants are harming the economy. While economists have found that undocumented workers lowered the wages of U.S. adults who did not have a high-school diploma, those states with a high immigrant population actually prospered because immigrants do not compete with skilled workers. In those areas, skilled native workers made a good wage and worked more hours, increasing productivity.

Americans businesses have also taken advantage of the undocumented. Certain industries, including food service, manufacturing, and meatpacking, rely on immigrant laborers, many of whom are in the country illegally. As a result, they are forced to take lower wages.

Other people, including many politicians and policy makers, suggest that unauthorized immigrants be deported. Some have even called for the government to build walls at the borders to keep people out. They also suggest reducing the number of legal immigrants who can come in and stay in the country, while refusing the undocumented a way to become citizens.

Ongoing Debate

As the refugee crisis of 2015—the largest since World War II—continues, the stresses will increase in the many countries, large and small, on the front line of the migration routes. Ongoing conflicts and persistent terrorism threats—perceived or real—will exacerbate the debate about how to solve the refugee problem. These conflicts will also affect people's attitude toward economic migration. Open borders to immigrants, according to many analysts, might seem like a luxury we can no longer afford.

That said, a person's drive to improve his or her chances for a better life—whether under the threat of civil war or grinding poverty at home—will not abate. The cultural connections, free exchange of information, and porous borders that developed along with other globalizing forces are likely to persist. Despite ongoing debates, the refugees' hopes and journeys—whether in the United States, Europe, Africa, or elsewhere—will continue.

Text-Dependent Questions

1. How many people have been displaced by war in 2014?
2. How many Syrian refugees did Germany expect to take in by the end of 2015?
3. How many refugees were admitted to the United Sates in 2014?

Research Projects

1. Print out a line map of the world. Use this United Nations Web site to research the countries with the highest number of fleeing refugees: http://www.unhcr.org/pages/49c3646c1d.html. Highlight those countries in different shades. Study the map. What can you conclude?
2. Research the Syrian civil war and write a report about its causes and the impact it has had on its people.

Educational Video

A World in Crisis
Page 48–49
Report from the United Nations High Commissioner for Refugees on the massive refugee crisis that began in 2014.
Published on YouTube by the UN Refugee Agency.
https://youtu.be/pxUpIjVdpRo.

LEFT: A street market in Paris—with a diverse crowd that typifies the capital of France, home to many immigrants throughout its modern history.

Timeline

1945	By the end of World War II, over 6 million Jews and others have been murdered by the Nazi regime in Germany.
	By the end of World War II, 60 million Europeans are displaced as a result of the war.
	More than 2.2 million Germans are forced to leave Czechoslovakia after the Czech government confiscates their property at the end of the war.
1947	India wins its independence from Britain, but it is partitioned when Indian Muslims establish their own state of Pakistan; nearly 12 million people resettle across the new borders.
	The Marshall Plan is established to provide U.S. financial support for Europe's economic recovery, in hopes of halting Soviet expansion as the Cold War begins.
1948	The nation of Israel is founded, providing a homeland to Jews, but uprooting Palestinians from their homes.
1949	Some 700,000 Palestinians leave towns and villages that are now occupied by Israel.
	The number of Braceros—Mexican workers invited to work in the United States—has increased from some 70,000 during World War II to 113,000.
1950	There are 3.5 million Jews in Europe, comparted to 9.5 in 1933, when Hitler came to power in Germany.
	The United Nations establishes the Office of the UN High Commissioner for Refugees (UNHCR).
1950s	Benefitting greatly from the Marshall Plan, West Germany's gross domestic product rises 8 percent each year, faster than anywhere else in Europe.
1950s–1960s	Labor migrants are welcomed into many European nations, including Indians and Pakistanis to Great Britain, and North Africans and Vietnamese to France.
1951	Six years after the end of World War II, one million European refugees have yet to resettle.
1953	As many as 170,000 Jewish refugees migrate to Israel; others move to Australia, New Zealand, South America, South Africa, and Mexico.
	After the Korean War ends, a 150-mile Demilitarized Zone (DMZ) is established, blocking travel and migration across the border.
	From 1945 until this year, some 900,000 North Koreans have migrated to South Korea.

1956	An anti-Soviet uprising in Budapest, Hungary, results in the death of thousands and some 250,000 Hungarians fleeing the country; it is the first refugee crisis handled by the UNHCR.
1960	Castro's revolution in Cuba in 1959 causes 163,000 refugees to leave for the United States, compared to 71,000 ten years prior.
1961	By this year, when the Berlin Wall is constructed, some 3.8 million East Germans have moved to West Germany.
	Germany and Turkey sign an agreement to increase the number of Turkish workers allowed into Germany.
1962	Algeria secures its independence from France after a lengthy war; thousands of refugees swarm into neighboring Tunisia and Morocco, living in tent cities in the desert.
1964	By the time the Bracero Program ends, 4.6 million Mexican laborers have come to work in the United States.
1970	The Bhola cyclone hits East Pakistan (now Bangladesh) and the east coast of India, resulting in a massive number of deaths and displaced persons.
1973	Between 1955 and this year, 14 million guest workers have come to Germany from Italy, Morocco, Portugal, and Turkey, which has contributed the majority.
1974	*The Gulag Archipelago* by Soviet dissident Aleksandr Solzhenitsyn is published outside of the Soviet Union; he is forced into internal exile.
	World-renowned ballet dancer Mikhail Baryshnikov defects to the West.
1975	From the end of World War II until now, Australia has welcomed 3 million people, including many from Eastern Europe.
	At the end of the Vietnam War, the North Vietnamese will take over South Vietnam, resulting in the forced relocation of tens of thousands of people and a mass exodus of "boat people."
1980	Fidel Castro allows all Cubans wishing to migrate to the United States to leave in what comes to be called the Mariel Boatlift.
1985	The Schengen Agreement is signed, making it easier for Europeans to migrate from one European country to another.
	The United Nations Environment Program defines *environmental refugees* "as those people who have been forced to leave their traditional habitat, temporarily or permanently, because of a marked environmental disruption."
1989	The Berlin Wall comes down and East Germany announces it will open its border and allow its citizens to travel freely to the West.

Timeline (continued)

1995	At the end of the Bosnian civil war, part of a larger conflict in Yugoslavia, the number of refugees, including those displaced within the country, numbers 2 million.
2001	Following the September 11 terrorist attacks in the United States, immigration will drop off considerably over the next fifteen years.
2004	An earthquake under the Indian Ocean creates a huge tsunami that results in 228,000 dead or missing and 1.7 million displaced and homeless in Asia; Indonesia is hit the hardest.
2005	Hurricane Katrina devastates parts of low-lying New Orleans and other cities along the Gulf of Mexico, resulting in 2,000 dead or missing and displacing more than a million people.
2007	Unauthorized immigration to the United States peaks at 12.2 million, then drops sharply between 2007 and 2009 (during the Great Recession), and continues to decrease after that.
2013	From 1990, after the Berlin Wall falls, until this year, the population of West Germany has grown by 6.7 percent, while the population of East Germany has dropped by 13.5 percent.
	Typhoon Haiyan devastates the Philippines, killing more than 6,000 people and displacing some 4.4 million people.
2014	Some 19.3 million people are forced to flee their homes because of climate- and weather-related disasters.
	In Bangladesh, more than 200,000 people are temporarily displaced by floods and landslides during the region's rainy season.
	There are close to 1.1 million UN-registered refugees in Lebanon at the end of the year, compared to Lebanon's population of 4.4 million in 2011, at the start of the Syrian civil war.
	Remittances from immigrants to their homes in India total $70 billion, in China $64 billion, and in the Philippines $28 billion.
2015	The agreement emerging from the global climate talks in Paris is criticized for not including a category of "climate refugees" who have the same rights as other refugees.
	With 4.1 million people fleeing, the Syrian civil war contributes to the worst refugee crises since World War II; Germany accepts 800,000 refugees, the most of any European country.
	In another part of the refugee crisis, some 700 Africans drown in the Mediterranean Sea as they try migrate to Europe in hopes of escaping famine, drought, and political turmoil.

Further Research

BOOKS

Dalton, Dave. *Refugees & Asylum Seekers*. Chicago: Heinemman Library, 2006.

Hayes, Patrick J., ed. *The Making of Modern Immigration: An Encyclopedia of People and Ideas*. Santa Barbara, CA: ABC-CLIO., 2012.

Khan, Yasmin. *India at War: The Subcontinent and the Second World War*. New York: Oxford University Press, 2015.

UNHCR. *The State of the World's Refugees 2012: In Search of Solidarity*. New York: Oxford University Press, 2012.

ONLINE

Human Rights Watch: http://www.hrw.org/topic/refugees.

International Committee of the Red Cross: https://www.icrc.org/en.

Norwegian Refugee Council: http://www.nrc.no.

UNHCR: http://www.unhcr.org/pages/49c3646c2.html.

U.S. Committee for Refugees and Immigrants: http://www.refugees.org/?referrer=https://www.google.com/.

NOTE TO EDUCATORS: This book contains both imperial and metric measurements as well as references to global practices and trends in an effort to encourage the student to gain a worldly perspective. We, as publishers, feel it's our role to give young adults the tools they need to thrive in a global society.

Index

Italicized page numbers refer to illustrations

A

Africa 11, 21–22, 27, 44–46, *45*
Alaska 44
Algeria 22, 27
American Joint Distribution Committee 17
artistic freedom 34–35
Asia 13, 17, 20, 41, *43*
Assad, Bashir 46
asylum 9–10, 35, 49, 51, *52*
Australia 18, 20–21, 38, 44
Avial, Collete 10

B

Bangladesh 11, 42, 46, *46*
Baryshnikov, Mikhail 35
Berlin Wall 25, *36*, 36–37
Bhola cyclone (Bangladesh, 1970) 42
Bosnian civil war 11, *11*
Bracero Program 27–29
brain drain 51
Britain 9, 17–21, 25, 27, 38
Burundi 22

C

Cambodia 37
Canada 9, 21, 38, 42
capitalism 25
CARE International 42
Carter, Jimmy 37
Castro, Fidel 29, *29*
China 17, 33, 50
Chinese Exclusion Act (1882) 53, *53*
civil rights movement 53
civil war 9–11, *11*, 27, 33, 54. *See also* war
climate and environmental refugees 12, 42
climate change 11–12, 42–46, *44–45*, *46*
Cold War 19–20, 25, 27, 33, 36, 53
colonialism 21–22, 27
concentration camps 17, *18*. *See also* World War II
Cuba 29, *29–30*
cultural connections 14, 49–50, 54
Czechoslovakia 19, 25

D

deportation 54
desertification 44–46, *45*. *See also* climate change
Displaced Persons Act (1948) 18
drought 12, 44–46, *45*, 46

E

earthquakes 42
Eastern Europe 13, 17, 20, 25
East Germany 25, 37. *See also* Germany
economic downturns 51
economic growth 14, 18, 25–27, *26*, 29–30, 50–51, 53
economic immigration 12–13, 22, 25–27, 29, 34, 54
education 14, 51, 53
Environmental Justice Foundation 12
Ethiopia 44
ethnic cleansing 11
ethnic tensions 11, 20, 22, 26–27
Europe 13, 19–20, *24*, 25–27, 45–46
European Economic Community 27
European Union (EU) 9, 27, 51–52

F

famine 44–46, 49
Farm Security Administration *28*
Feltsman, Vladimir 35
floods 42, 46, *46*
fossil fuels 43. *See also* global warming
France 9, 17, 27, 45, 52, *54*
Francis (pope) 46

G

genocide 11
Germany 9, 13, 19, 25–27, *26*, *36*, 36–37, 51–52
globalization 41, 49–51, 54
global warming 11–12, 42–46
Gorbachev, Mikhail 37
Great Britain. *See* Britain
Greece *8*, 9
greenhouse gases 43. *See also* global warming

60   MIGRATION AND REFUGEES

guest worker programs 26–29, *28*
Guevara, Ernesto Ché 29
Gulag Archipelago, The (Solzhenitsyn) 35
Guterres, Antonio 14, *14*

H

Haiti 42
Herzog, Isaac 10, *10*
Ho Chi Minh 37
Holocaust 10, *16,* 17–18, *18. See also* World War II
Holocaust Memorial Museum (Washington, D.C.) 17
Hungary 19, 21, *22,* 52
Hurricane Katrina 42–43

I

immigration: culture and assimilation 14, 49–50, 54; economic motivation 12–13, 22, 25–27, 29, 34, 54; environmental impact 13–14; and ethnic tensions 11, 20, 22, 26–27; guest worker programs 26–29; political motivation 11, 35, 49; political policies and backlash 51–54; quotas 18, 53; and receiver countries 14, 50–51; and religious violence 20–21; and remittances 50, *50,* 51
Immigration and Nationality Act (1965) 53
independence movements 21–22, 27, 37
India 20–21, *21,* 27, 42, 50
Indonesia 42, *43*
infrastructure and social services 13–14, *26,* 51
intellectual migration 50–51
International Refugee Organization 17
Islamic State of Iraq and Syria (ISIS) 49, 52. *See also* terrorism
Israel 10, 18–19, *19,* 35–36
Italy *24,* 45

J

Japan 42
Jewish Brigade Group 18
Jewish migration 10, *16,* 17–18, 35–36. *See also* Holocaust, World War II
Jinnah, Muhammad Ali 20
Jordan 10

K

Korea *32,* 33–34, *34*
Kurdi, Aylan and Abdullah 9, 49, 52

L

labor force 14, 27–29, 51, 53
Laos 37
Latin America 27–30
League of Nations 18
Lebanon 14

M

Maastricht Treaty (1992) 27
Mariel boatlift 29, 52
Marshall, George C. 25
Marshall Plan *24,* 25
Mexico 13, 27, *28,* 28–29
Middle East 10–11, 14, 18–19, *19,* 35–36, 46. *See also* Syria
migrant farm workers *12,* 27–29, *28*
migration routes 54
Mondale, Walter 37

N

National Front (France) 52
nationality quotas 53. *See also* immigration
natural disasters 11, 41–43
Netherlands 27
New Orleans 42–43
New York City 44
New Zealand 18, 44
Ngo Dinh Diem 37
Nigeria 45
Norwegian Refugee Council 11
Nureyev, Rudolf 35

O

Operación Manos a la Obra (Operation Bootstrap) 29
Organisation for Economic Co-operation and Development 51

Index (continued)

P
Pakistan 20–21, 27, 42
Palestine *16,* 18–19, *19*
Paris 52, *54*
Philippines *40,* 41, 50
Poland 19, 21, 25
policy debate 51–54
political freedom 34–35
poverty 12–13, 22, 25–27, 29, 34, 54
Puerto Rico 29

R
racism 53
refugee crisis 18, 49, 51–54. See also immigration
refuseniks 35–36
religious violence 20–21, *21*
remittances 50, *50,* 51
Romania 10, 19
Rwanda 22

S
Saab, Elias Bou 14
San Bernardino 52–53
Sarajevo *11*
Schengen Agreement (1985) 27
September 11, 2001 terrorist attack 52
Sikhs 21
Six Days War 35
skilled workers 53
Slovakia 52
smugglers 9
social market economy 25
social services 13–14
Solzhenitsyn, Aleksandr 35, *35*
Soviet Union 19, 21, *22,* 25, 33–37
spies 35
Sri Lanka 42
Stern, Caryl M. 9
Sweden 52, *52*
Syria *8,* 9–10, *13,* 14, 46, *48,* 49, *52,* 52–54

T
terrorism 49, 52–54
Truman, Harry S. 18, 20, *20*
tsunami (Indian Ocean, 2004) 42, *43*
Turkey 9, 26, 52, *52*
Tuvalu 44, *44*
Typhoon Haiyan (Philippines, 2013) *40,* 41

U
undocumented workers 53–54
UNHCR (United Nations High Commissioner for Refugees) 10, 14, 21–22, *48*
United Nations 22, 37, 42, 49
United Nations Climate Change Conference (COP21, Paris, 2015) 42
United Nations Environment Program 42
United Nations Relief and Rehabilitation Administration (UNRRA) 17
United States: and Cuban and Latin America migration *12,* 27–30, *30*; and economic immigration 9, 12–13; immigration levels and political debate 50–54, *53*; and Korean War 33–34; natural disaster relief efforts 42–43; and political refugees 21–22, 34, *38*; and post-World War II migration 17–19, 25; and Syrian refugee crisis 9; and Vietnam War 37–38, *38*
United States Fund for UNICEF 9

V
Vietnam 27, 37–38, *38*

W
war 9–11, *11,* 13–14, 27, *32,* 33–38, 46, 49–54. See also World War II
weather-related tragedies 11, *40,* 41–43, *43–44,* 46, *46*
West Germany 25–26, *26,* 37. See also Germany
World War II 10, 17–21, 25, 27, 36–37

X
xenophobia 51–53

Y
Yugoslavia 11, 21, 25

Photo Credits

Page number	Page location	Archive/Photographer
8	Top	Shutterstock/De Visu
10	Middle	Wikimedia Commons/crystalarts
11	Top	Shutterstock/Northfoto
12	Bottom	Shutterstock/rightdx
13	Bottom	iStock/AhmadSabra
14	Top	Wikimedia Commons /U.S. Mission Photo by Eric Bridiers
16	Top	Wikimedia Commons /KLUGER ZOLTAN
18	Bottom	Wellcome Library, London
19	Top	Wikimedia Commons/Eldan David
20	Bottom	Library of Congress
21	Top	Wikimedia Commons/Photo Division, Govt. of India
22	Bottom	Shutterstock/Everett Historical
24	Top	Wikimedia Commons /National Archives and Records Administration
26	Top	iStock/eddl
28	Top	Library of Congress
29	Top	Wikimedia Commons
30	Bottom	U.S. Coast Guard
32	Top	Wikimedia Commons
34	Top	Wikimedia Commons /Edward N. Johnson, U.S. Army Public Affairs Officer
35	Bottom	Wikimedia Commons/Dutch National Archives
36	Top	Wikimedia Commons/Daderot
38	Bottom	Wikimedia Commons /PH2 Phil Eggman
40	Top	Wikimedia Commons/Trocaire
43	Bottom	Wikimedia Commons/AusAID
44	Top	Wikimedia Commons /Gabriella Jacobi
45	Bottom	Wikimedia Commons/Oxfam East Africa
46	Bottom	Wikimedia Commons/Amanda Jennings, AusAID
48	Top	Shutterstock/Photoman29
50	Bottom	Wikimedia Commons
52	Top	iStock/KIVILCIM PINAR
53	Top	Library of Congress
54	Bottom	Wikimedia Commons/David Monniaux
Cover	Top	Shutterstock/Everett Historical
Cover	Left	Shutterstock/Lukasz Z
Cover	Right	Shutterstock/rmnoa357

About the Author and Advisor

Series Advisor

Ruud van Dijk teaches the history of international relations at the University of Amsterdam, the Netherlands. He studied history at Amsterdam, the University of Kansas, and Ohio University, where he obtained his Ph.D. in 1999. He has also taught at Carnegie Mellon University, Dickinson College, and the University of Wisconsin-Milwaukee, where he also served as editor at the Center for 21st Century Studies. He has published on the East-West conflict over Germany during the Cold War, the controversies over nuclear weapons in the 1970s and 1980s, and on the history of globalization. He is the senior editor of the *Encyclopedia of the Cold War* (2008) produced with MTM Publishing and published by Routledge.

Author

John Perritano is an award-winning journalist, writer, and editor from Southbury, Connecticut, who has written numerous articles and books on a variety of subjects including history, politics, and culture for such publishers as Mason Crest, National Geographic, Scholastic, and *Time/Life*. His articles have appeared on Discovery.com, Popular Mechanics.com, and other magazines and websites. He holds a master's degree in American History from Western Connecticut State University.